FLOW DISCOVERY JOURNAL
& COLORING BOOK

Daily Questions
to Spark Your Beginner's Mind

– for children ages 5 to 105 –

CARMEN VIKTORIA GAMPER

ILLUSTRATED BY SYBILLE KRAMER

Flow Discovery Journal and Coloring Book: Daily Questions to Spark Your Beginner's Mind – for Children Ages 5 to 105

Copyright © 2020 by Carmen Viktoria Gamper
New Learning Culture Publishing. All Rights Reserved.

Illustrations: Sybille Kramer
Back cover photo by Robert Hickling

ISBN: 978-1-7347970-5-3 (paperback)

1. Activity Book 2. Coloring Book 3. Parent Participation in Education

*Any action you take upon the information in this book is strictly at your own risk, and we will not be liable for any losses or damages in connection with the use of this book. No parts of this book may be reproduced and transmitted in any form and by any means without the written permission of the publisher, except in the case of brief quotations used in book reviews and critical articles.
For permission requests write to:
Info@NewLearningCulture.com*

NEW LEARNING CULTURE PUBLISHING
San Francisco, California
www.NewLearningCulture.com

Dedicated to you

{your name here}

_____

INTRODUCTION

Hello you!

There are 7 billion people on this planet. You are one of them, and there is no one like you!

You have unique thoughts, opinions, likes and dislikes. Your mind is like a secret world inside of you. It can create things no one else can. But how well do you know this secret world? In these pages, you will find questions and activities designed to open your mind and learn more about yourself.

We often take our mind for granted. Instead of thinking our own thoughts, we believe what others tell us. Instead of remaining curious, we pretend to know everything. But no one ever discovered something interesting by knowing everything! The best inventions were created because someone asked a question, and they explored their secret inner world to find a unique answer.

The *Flow Discovery Journal* will inspire curiosity and original thoughts—the kinds of thoughts only you can think.
By pondering even the simplest questions, you will get to know yourself in new, exciting ways. There are no wrong answers. There is no way to make a mistake. There is only exploration and discovery!

Everyone's mind works differently.
What makes you intelligent isn't the same as what makes someone else intelligent.
In fact, according to the developmental psychologist Howard Gardner, there are nine types of intelligence. For the purpose of knowing yourself fully, three more have been added to this book, making 12 kinds of intelligence in total. By understanding all of them, we can know ourselves better.
Do any of these ways of thinking sound like you?

12 KINDS OF INTELLIGENCE

Practical Intelligence

Practical intelligence is the ability to find a solution to a problem and achieve a desired result. When you think this way, you know how to address life's big and small challenges. For instance, builders find solutions for us to live comfortably; chefs and farmers find solutions for us to eat good food. When you can fix a broken pen, repair a car, or find a way to cross a river, then you have practical intelligence.

Visionary Intelligence

Visionary intelligence is the ability to imagine, visualize, and dream of something that does not exist in the world. Inventors, explorers, and people who likes to improve life use visionary intelligence. You might imagine being an ameba and writing a story about its life, or you invent a simple microscope. By imagining, inventing, and planning, you strengthen your visionary intelligence.

Linguistic Intelligence

Linguistic intelligence enables you to understand and use spoken and written words in useful, fun ways. Writers, journalists, poets, songwriters, comedians, and teachers all use linguistic intelligence. When you express yourself through words, poetry, rhymes, songs, stories, and plays, you hone your linguistic intelligence.

Mathematical Intelligence

Mathematical intelligence is the ability to use numbers and other measurements to engage with your surroundings. Through counting, playing with numbers, solving mathematical problems, measuring things, collecting data, or identifying recurring patterns and shapes, you sharpen your mathematical intelligence.

Spatial Intelligence

Spatial intelligence is the ability to picture something in your imagination exactly as you've seen it before. You might enjoy drawing, making miniature models, or creating designs on a computer. When you remember a walk in the city, when you can rebuild a block tower the way you did the day before, or when you plan a garden, you're practicing your spatial intelligence.

Bodily-Kinesthetic Intelligence

Bodily-kinesthetic intelligence is the ability to move your body gracefully and efficiently, and to handle objects skillfully. People who love dancing, playing instruments, horseback riding, skiing, and all other sports and hands-on activities use the intelligence of their bodies. If you enjoy moving and using your body and hands, then you exercise bodily-kinesthetic intelligence.

Musical Intelligence

Musical intelligence is the ability to create, practice, and enjoy music, sounds, and rhythms. If you like listening to music, singing, humming melodies, whistling, or simply tapping your fingers rhythmically, you use your musical intelligence.

Empathic Intelligence

Empathic intelligence is the ability to understand, imagine, and feel what another person or an animal is experiencing. When you read a story and feel the character's pain and happiness, or when you pretend to be someone else when playing, you use your empathic intelligence. People with empathetic intelligence often want to help others.

Introspective Intelligence

Introspective intelligence is the ability to know yourself. It requires self-reflection, and a desire to know what you like and don't like, and why. People with introspective intelligence know that who they are isn't fixed—they are always growing, changing, and learning new things.

Naturalist Intelligence

Naturalistic intelligence is an interest in the natural world, plants, animals, and their diverse habitats. People with this intelligence track animals and identify their footprints, listen for birdsongs, camp outside, and observe insects. If you love wild animals, taking care of a pet, observing ants, naming plants on your nature walk, or growing plants, then you have naturalistic intelligence.

Existential Intelligence

Existential intelligence is the desire to ask questions about humanity: Why are we here? Where are we going? What is happiness? Why aren't more people happy? You might ask questions about the ethics of being human, or learn about different cultures or religions. Philosophers, psychologists, and everyone who likes to ponder a human's place in the universe use existential intelligence.

Intuitive Intelligence – The Flow State

Intuitive intelligence is the ability to do a task really well without having to think about it. Intuitive intelligence often comes in the form of a flow state. In a flow state, people don't think in words, but trust their body's intelligence and their whole being to guide their choices. Intuitive intelligence includes "Aha!" moments, and the feeling of being at the right place at the right time. When you focus on a hands-on activity, forget about time, and feel fulfilled, you are using intuitive intelligence.

~~~~~~~~~~~~~~~~~~~~

Throughout this journal, you will discover which intelligences come easily to you, and which ones you want to practice. This is your special journey of self-discovery—use it however you want!

There are different ways you can answer the questions. For example, you can write your answer with words. If you prefer writing on lines, you can use the dots on both sides of the pages to draw lines
between the points with a ruler:

Or, you can draw your answer with a pencil or colored pencils. Whether you answer one question a day or two—whether you complete this journal by yourself or with a loved one — by the end, you will feel like you know yourself better. And I hope you will know that you have something unique to offer to the world. That offering is precious and worth exploring!

Get your pencil ready, turn the page, and set out on an expedition into the secret world inside you, and the world all around!

DAY   1

Imagine tomorrow is one of
the best days of your life!
What would you do?
Draw or describe it here, please:

DAY 2

What are your favorite books?

DAY 2

Can you imagine writing
one or more books?
What would it be about?
Draw or describe them here, please:

DAY 3

Have you ever looked through
a microscope? What did you see?
If you haven't, what do you imagine seeing?

DAY 3

Did you know that your body
is made of trillions of cells?
Imagine you could talk to all of them.
What would you say?

DAY 4 _____

Write a letter to yourself in the future. Pretend you will read it many years from now.

What would you say to yourself? What would you like to remember?

Dear_____,

DAY 4

DAY 5

Have you ever built something
that was taller than you? What was it?
A snowman, a blocks tower, or a building?
If you haven't, what would it be?

DAY 5

Color in and add your own details to the drawing

DAY 6

Look around the room, and outside the window. What do you see that would take a long time to count? Is there anything that is completely uncountable?

Imagine you needed exactly 36 cherries for a special dining table decoration. What's (for you) the fastest way or your preferred way to count the cherries?

DAY 6

How many times do you
see 4 of something
in your room,
in the kitchen,
or outside?

DAY 7

Have you ever dug your hands into dark, soft soil? How did it feel? If you haven't, would you like to? If not, why?

DAY 7

Have you ever planted a seed
and watched it grow?

DAY 8

Do you know what the girl on the drawing is using? How could you find out about this?

DAY 8

Can you imagine building one of these?
What would you need to build it,
and how would you do it?

What would you use it for?

DAY 9

Which items make you especially happy? Are there certain instruments, books, toys, flowers, foods, crystals, scents, pictures, art supplies, clothes, or other things that lift your spirits?

DAY 9

Do you sometimes have a really bad day,
when you just don't feel good?
What do you do to comfort yourself?

DAY 10

Do you know what the
object in this drawing is?
Have you ever seen one of
these outdated clocks?

Can you think of other things
that were normal many years ago,
but are rarely seen today?

DAY 10

Do you know someone who is much, much older than you? Who is it, and what do you like about them?

DAY 11

When have you last played with water?
Where were you, and how did it feel?
Could you play with water today?

DAY 11

Have you ever noticed the patterns
water makes when it flows?
How it sparkles, sprinkles,
meanders, and spirals?
You could draw some of those
patterns here:

DAY 12

Do you like when your things are in order,
with specific places for each thing?
Or do you prefer when your things
are a little messy? Why do you prefer
one over the other?

DAY 12

DAY 13 _____

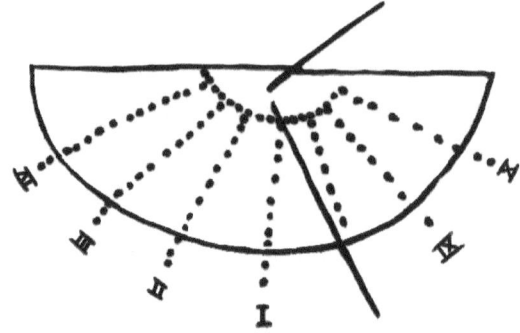

Have you ever seen a sundial?
Can you guess how it works?

Could you imagine creating one?
How would you do it?

DAY 13

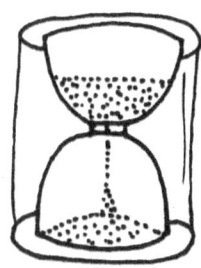

This is a drawing of an hourglass. The sand on top takes exactly one hour to get through the narrow passage in the middle.

Can you invent another unusual way to measure time?

DAY 14 _____

DAY 14

What is your favorite meal? Draw it below, or write down the recipe:

DAY 15 _____

Look around your home.
Do you see something that you made
with your own hands? What is it?

What is something else you'd like
to make for your home, or to play with?

DAY 15

DAY 16

Have you ever been barefoot...
{color the star next to the words if your answer is yes}

☆ on the beach
☆ on moss
☆ on pebbles
☆ on dry leaves
☆ on velvet
☆ on rocks
☆ on silk
☆ in the water
☆ on grass
☆ on flower petals
☆ on metal
☆ in your socks
☆ in the mud
☆ in the snow

Where did you place your toe?
I would love to know!

_____ DAY 16

Color in & add your own details to the drawing

DAY 17

What are your favorite flowers?
What do you feel
when you see and smell them?

_____ DAY 17

Which kinds of flowers have you smelled with your own nose?

-
-
-
-
-
-
-

Where would you go to learn more about flowers?

-
-
-
-
-
-
-

DAY 18

Do you like adventures?
Make a list of the things or places
you would like to see, discover,
and explore:

DAY 18

Color in & add your own details to the drawing

DAY 19 _____

Can you imagine being
as small as a butterfly?
What would you do? Where would you go?

DAY 19

Do you have a superpower?
Can you imagine having one?
What is it? What will you do?

DAY 20

What are your personal treasures?
Are there special places
where you put them?

DAY 20

Color in and add your own details to the drawing

DAY 21

Did you know that you can solve multiplication problems by counting points where lines meet?

For instance 14 x 12 =

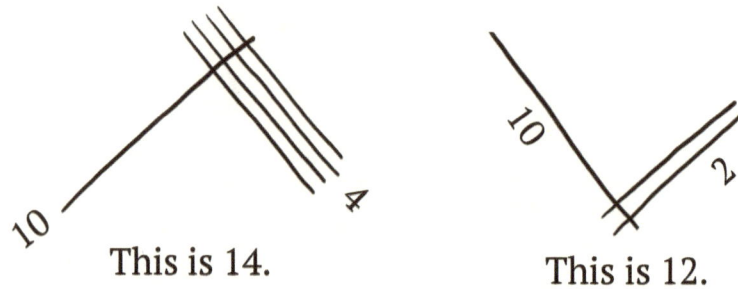

This is 14.   This is 12.

Combine the two drawings. Then, count the intersecting points:

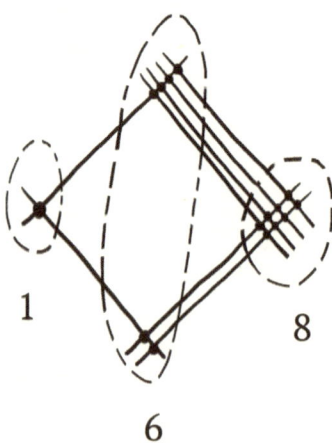

The result of this multiplication is 168.

_____ DAY 21

Now, you can try:
23 x 32 =

DAY 22 _____

Have you ever
seen a rainbow in the sky?
Or have you seen one
somewhere else?
Can you draw a rainbow here?

DAY 22

What is your favorite
color combination? Draw a rainbow,
or anything else,
using your favorite colors:

DAY 23

How many instruments do you know?
Can you list them here?

DAY 23

If you could play any instrument,
which one would you pick and why?

DAY 24

Have you ever crafted something fun from recycled materials, such as:

☆ an aluminum foil robot,

☆ a sock doll,

☆ a cork boat,

☆ a paper airplane,

☆ or a shoebox aquarium?

If you were to make something,
you would need materials such as paper,
tape, glue, scissors, shoeboxes, egg cartons,
aluminum foil, gift packaging material,
a needle and thread, wine corks, a sock,
buttons, plastic bottles, and bottle caps.

DAY 24

You could create something that...

☆ moves with the wind

☆ flies in the air

☆ floats on the water

☆ makes you smile

☆ makes you laugh out loud

☆ you can give as a gift

☆ you can hang on your wall

☆ you can wear as a necklace

☆ is a game you can play

☆ makes sounds or noises

☆ doesn't make any sense at all

☆ _____

☆ _____

DAY 25 _____

Can you imagine grownups as children?
Imagine a grownup you love
as a child.
How does that feel?

DAY 25

Imagine a grownup you don't like very much as a child.
How does that feel? Do you like them more?

Have you ever asked grownups about the games they played when they were children?
List and describe them here:

DAY 26 _____

Have you ever
changed your mind about something?
Maybe you tried something
you thought was scary,
and it was fun?
Or maybe you started
liking a food you used to dislike?

DAY 26

Color in & add your own details to the drawing

DAY 27 _____

Please make a list
of all the things
you love about yourself.
Please don't hold back,
but brag about yourself:

-
-
-
-
-
-
-
-
-
-
-
-
-
-
-
-
-

DAY 27

Please make a list
of all the things
you would like to learn,
even those you think you might
never be able to learn:

-
-
-
-
-
-
-
-
-
-
-
-
-
-
-

DAY 28 _____

Did you know that cats and dogs
speak different languages?
When dogs wag their tails it means
they are happy and excited.
But when cats wag their tails
it means they are anxious and annoyed.
This might be a reason
why cats and dogs often don't get along.

DAY 28

Have you ever had a conflict with someone because of a misunderstanding? If yes, what was it? How did you discover it was a misunderstanding?

{If not...that's amazing! I don't know anyone who had never had a conflict because of a misunderstanding. Congratulations!}

DAY 29 _____

What is your favorite kind of weather, and why?

Have you ever walked in the rain without an umbrella? If yes, did you like it? If no, would you like to try it?

Have you ever jumped into a puddle? If yes, how did that feel? If no, why not?

DAY 29

DAY 30

Have you ever heard music
that you could feel in your body,
and you simply had to dance?

_____ DAY 30

Listen to your favorite music
and draw it here:

DAY 31

What is something magical
that has happened in your life?

DAY 31

For instance, have you ever run into someone right when you were thinking about them? Have you ever unexpectedly found something that you needed or wished for?

DAY 32

If you could be any animal,
what animal would you like to be,
and why? Please draw or write your answer:

Pretend being that animal for a little while!
How does it feel?

DAY 32

What animals would
your parents or friends be?

DAY 33 _____

Have you ever looked at the stars for a long time? How did that feel? What were you thinking?

Have you ever imagined infinity, such as infinite stars, infinite sand, infinite leaves? How did that feel?

DAY 33

Color in & add your own details to the drawing

DAY 34

Have you ever invented a song,
sung a melody,
or made sounds and noises that
no one had ever heard before?
Could you do that now?

DAY 34

Have you ever created something
that makes a fun noise,
like a sand shaker,
rice rattle,
or bucket drum?
Could you create or imagine
a new instrument right now?

DAY 35

Have you ever had
a wonderfully cozy place for yourself?
Maybe it was a fort,
or a reading corner with pillows,
or a window seat with a great view.

Describe or draw the perfect
cozy place for you:

DAY 35

What are some activities
that light up your spirit or relax you,
or give you an inner peace
that feels like home?
{Circle the items on the list below and add your own}

- ☆ Playing alone or with others
- ☆ Cooking a special meal
- ☆ Eating with family and friends
- ☆ Reading a book or watching a movie
- ☆ Painting, drawing, writing, and journaling
- ☆ Moving your body, dancing, or sports
- ☆ Experiencing nature, gardening
- ☆ Listening to music, singing, making music
- ☆ Crafting and creating objects
- ☆ Pondering the mysteries of the universe
- ☆ Having an inspiring conversation
- ☆ Taking a bath
- ☆
- ☆
- ☆
- ☆

DAY 36

If you could invite anyone in the world
to a tea party, who would you choose?
This guest could be a friend,
or a person who lived a long time ago,
or an imaginary person,
or a magical creature
such as a fairy godmother,
or even an animal friend.

Who would be your guest,
and what would you talk about?

DAY 36

DAY 37 _____

Make a long list of things
you could do when you are bored:

- ·
- ·
- ·
- ·
- ·
- ·
- ·
- ·
- ·
- ·
- ·
- ·
- ·
- ·
- ·
- ·
- ·
- ·
- ·
- ·

DAY 37

Have you ever made yourself
laugh or smile?
Have you ever made someone else
laugh or smile?

DAY 38 _____

Have you ever seen the moon
when it is full, when it is waning,
and when it is waxing?

Please draw all the different
moon shapes you have seen:

_____ DAY 38

Isn't it interesting that the full moon
looks as if it was as big as the sun,
yet the sun is about 400 times
larger than the moon and
about 400 times farther away.

Do you think that's a coincidence,
or could this have a deeper meaning?

DAY 39 _____

Have you ever pretended
to be someone else?
Who did you pretend to be and why?

_____ DAY 39

Try it now!
How does it feel to be…

- ☆ a circus director
- ☆ a clown
- ☆ a lion
- ☆ a detective
- ☆ an astronaut
- ☆ an explorer
- ☆ a mother or father
- ☆ a ballet dancer
- ☆ a scientist
- ☆ a fireman
- ☆ a hairdresser
- ☆ a musician
- ☆ a prince or princess
- ☆ a robber
- ☆ an angel
- ☆ a teacher
- ☆ a police man
- ☆

DAY 40 _____

Some people remember being a baby. What is your earliest memory?

DAY 40

What is something you wished you remembered about being a baby?

DAY 41 _____

Do you prefer this, that, or both...?
{Color the stars next to the words if your answer is yes}

☆ to be on stage ········ OR ········ ☆ to be in the audience

☆ to write ············ OR ················ ☆ to draw and color

☆ to sing ···················· OR ···················· ☆ to dance

☆ walk ···················· OR ···················· ☆ run

☆ jump ···················· OR ···················· ☆ crawl

☆ watch ···················· OR ···················· ☆ listen

☆ bike ···················· OR ···················· ☆ drive

☆ indoors ···················· OR ···················· ☆ outdoors

☆ talk ···················· OR ···················· ☆ listen

☆ loud ···················· OR ···················· ☆ quiet

☆ sweet ················ OR ························ ☆ salty

☆ cats ···················· OR ···················· ☆ dogs

☆ apples ···················· OR ···················· ☆ oranges

☆ getting up early ············· OR ············· ☆ sleeping in

☆ only a few people ············· OR ············· ☆ many people together

DAY 41

Color in & add your own details to the drawing

DAY 42

Have you ever heard of Braille language? People who know Braille read by moving their fingertips across patterns of raised dots on a page, instead of using their eyes.

DAY 42

Some games to play:

Prepare different kinds of foods, such as strawberries, carrots, bananas, and nuts. Blindfold yourself and try to figure out which is which only by tasting them.

Prepare a bag with a variety of little items such as a toy car, a pencil, a spoon, an eraser, and other small things you find, then blindfold yourself and guess which is which by using your fingers.

Find a friend to play this game: Draw a word on their back using your finger, and have them guess what you wrote.

DAY 43 _____

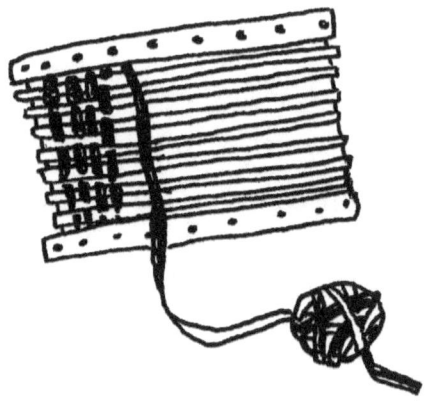

Do you know what this drawing is?
Many of our clothes and fabrics are made
with a bigger,
more complicated version of this.

Have you ever seen or worked
with a hand weaving loom?

DAY 43

Try crafting a simple loom.
You will need yarn
and a piece of cardboard
that is about the size
you want for your fabric.
Did you try? How did it go?

DAY 44 _____

How do you feel
when you do something well?
Make a list of all the things
you can do well:

-
-
-
-
-
-
-
-
-
-
-
-
-
-
-
-

-
-
-
-
-
-
-
-
-
-
-
-
-
-
-
-

DAY 44

DAY 45 _____

Have you ever played pretend sword fighting? If yes, did you enjoy it? If no, would you like to try it? Or, do you prefer not to try it?

DAY 45

Do you think boys/men and girls/women
are very different?
How are they different?

What things do boys/men and girls/women
have in common?

DAY 46 _____

Are there some thing you
weren't able to do last year
but you can do them this year?
Why can you do them now?
Write or draw your list:

DAY 46

Color in & add your own details to the drawing

DAY 47

Have you ever created a puzzle,
or could you imagine creating one?

.   .

.   .

.   .

.   .

.   .

Here is how you can create
a jigsaw puzzle: Draw a picture,
or find a photo,
and cut it in manageable pieces.
Then put it back together.

DAY 47

Here is how you can create
a word-find puzzle:
In the space below,
write words horizontally, vertically, and
diagonally, and fill the empty spaces in with
random letters. Now find the words!

DAY 48 _____

Have you ever wished you could fly like a bird?
Where would you go? What would you discover? How would you feel?

 DAY 48

Did you know,
you don't have to believe
all of your thoughts?
If you think something you don't like,
you can ask yourself,
how else could I think about this?

DAY 49 _____

Let's do some drawing exercises!

1. Try to draw a perfect circle:

2. Now try to draw a perfect circle with the hand you don't usually use:

3. Try to draw two circles using your right and left hand at the same time:

DAY 49

How many different images
can be made with a circle?
Draw as many as you can!
Here are two examples:

DAY 50 _____

This is not a fox:

It is only a drawing of a fox.

The word "f o x" is not a fox.
It is only a word that describes a fox.

_____ DAY 50

What is a fox?

Spark your existential intelligence

DAY 51

Let's play with language!
Write down as many words as you
can think of that rhyme with "time."

Write down as many words as you
can think of that make you happy:

DAY 51

Now, try to write a poem that rhymes with
the words you just collected,
something like this:

I have a great time
eating ice cream
in the sunshine.

DAY 52

What would you do if you were president and could make new rules for the world?

DAY 52

What would you do,
if people asked you to
redesign the school system?
Imagine the school that
you would like to go to:

DAY 53 _____

Have you ever seen shapes in the clouds,
like an animal, spaceship, or something else?
If yes, which ones do you remember?
If not, please go watch the clouds as soon as
you can, and describe or draw them here:

DAY 53

DAY 54 _____

What makes a good friend?

DAY 54

Do you think you are a good friend?
If yes, why? If no, why?

Can you imagine being
a great friend to yourself?
What would you say to yourself?
What would you do for fun?

DAY 55 _____

This is a drawing of a compass. The needle always points to the magnetic North pole of the earth.

Explorers use compasses to determine their direction.

Would you be interested in learning how to use a compass? How could you go about that?

DAY 55

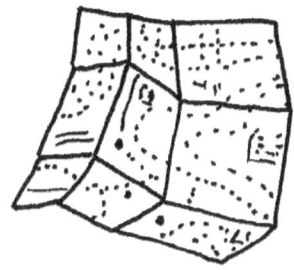

This is a drawing of a treasure map. You could hide a treasure in your home, and draw a map of where to find it.

You could give the map to a friend, and practice using a compass to find it. Here you can practice drawing your map:

DAY 56 _____

If you were a tree, what kind of tree would you like to be? Please draw or write it here:

DAY 56

Let's play pretend:
Stand up,
close your eyes,
and imagine for a moment
being that tree.
Feel your roots, feel your branches.
Is there wind, rain, sunshine?
How does it feel?

This is a drawing of the tree
that I would like to be.

DAY 57 _____

Look around your room and choose
a few objects. Do you know what
they are made of?
Do you know where they came from?
How would you find out?

．　　　　　　　　　　　　　．

．　　　　　　　　　　　　　．

．　　　　　　　　　　　　　．

．　　　　　　　　　　　　　．

．　　　　　　　　　　　　　．

．　　　　　　　　　　　　　．

DAY 57

Please list some of your things here,
and tell me what they are made of
and where they came from:

-
-
-
-
-
-
-
-
-
-
-
-
-
-
-
-
-

-
-
-
-
-
-
-
-
-
-
-
-
-
-
-
-
-

DAY 58 _____

What is your favorite wild animal, and why?

What do you know about this animal?
Where does it live? What does it eat?
What are the special things about this animal?

DAY 58

Imagine you could communicate
with that animal.
What would you talk about?
What would you do together?

Spark your empathic intelligence

DAY 59

Have you ever seen or walked a labyrinth?
Ancient wisdom says
labyrinths can help you find
your inner center.
Here is a special labyrinth.
Trace the black line with your finger
or with a pen, and after many rounds you will
arrive at the flower in the middle:

DAY 59

Here is how you can make
a simple labyrinth. You can draw it
or lay it out on the table with toothpicks
or on the ground with pebbles.
Can you find ways to make it bigger?
It doesn't have to be perfect to work.

1.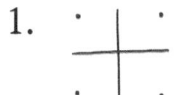

2.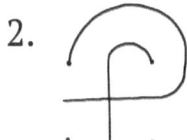

3.

4.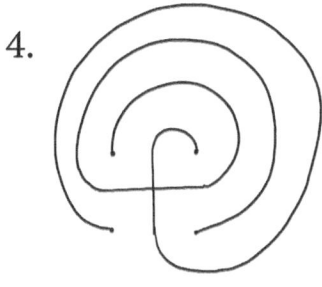

DAY 60 _____

Thank you for playing!
Here are the last questions:

Which questions did you like the most?

-
-
-

Which questions will you probably never forget?

-
-
-

Which questions have you or will you ask your friends?

-
-
-

_____ DAY 60

How about we celebrate now?
Let's be merry!
How would you like to celebrate?
{Please color the stars next to your yes .answers}

☆ dance party

☆ singing

☆ tea party

☆ lighting a candle

☆ hugging yourself or someone else

☆ getting flowers for yourself

☆ eating a special food

☆ inviting a friend over

☆ laughing out loud

☆ doing a happy dance

☆ going for a walk in nature

☆ _____

☆ _____

ABOUT THE AUTHOR

CARMEN VIKTORIA GAMPER is the author of *Flow To Learn: A 52 Week Parent's Guide to Recognize and Support Your Child's Flow State.*

Carmen is an educator, advisor, coach, and speaker for child-centered education. She became an expert on childhood flow states by supporting and witnessing hundreds of children learning on their own terms in carefully prepared, hands-on learning environments.

As founder of the New Learning Culture (NLC) program, she supports directors and staff of preschools and grade schools, parents and homeschooling families in safely offering child-directed, flow-rich learning environments.

Carmen created the *Flow Discovery Journal* to help children get away from screens, explore their own world, and eventually drop into the flow state of deep fulfilled focus –the optimal state for learning. The book is designed to be interesting for grown-up children, too!

Check out Carmen's website for more:
https://flowtolearn.com

ABOUT THE ILLUSTRATOR

SYBILLE KRAMER is the creator of the delightful drawings in Carmen's books. She is an artist and teacher from Alto Adige/South Tyrol, Italy. She is married and has two grown up sons and two dogs.

Sybille discovered her love for hands-on learning when her children went to a Rebeca Wild based, Montessori-inspired elementary school, and afterwards, when she homeschooled them through middle school.

Sybille turned her passion for hands-on learning into her profession and has since supported teachers and parents with the learning materials and classes she developed. She is one of driving forces of Homeschooling Italia, and also supports teachers in public schools.

Currently, Sybille is developing an online class together with Carmen to offer her delightful hands-on learning materials for preschool and grade school-aged children.

Check out her blog:
https://sybilletezzelekramer.wordpress.com/

THE PARENT's GUIDE: *FLOW TO LEARN*

*Flow To Learn: A 52-Week Parent's Guide
to Recognize and Support Your Child's Flow State
– the Optimal Condition for Learning*

FLOW TO LEARN is an uplifting, illustrated parent's guide, available in print and eBook, offering 52 weeks filled with practical suggestions and compassionate insights for creating independent play and learning opportunities for children.

Using practical, evidence-based tools from the fields of child development, psychology, and child-centered education, readers are guided step-by-step through the creation of simple hands-on activity stations that boost children's love for learning.

In these prepared environments, children naturally experience flow, the deeply focused state scientifically proven to be the optimal condition for learning.

Explore the 52 inspiring chapters to enrich every week of the year:

☆ Create activity stations in your home to free up your time while strengthening your child's intelligence and mental health
☆ Discover your child's vibrant inner world, and support them through the ups and downs of childhood
☆ See children as guides to your own flow state to bring more fun, meaning, and purpose into your lives

Each of the 52 Weeks of Flow To Learn offers two parts: First, readers find reflections and information about flow, then an array of practical suggestions, "Try This," on how to facilitate flow in life with children.

Some Weeks offer authentic and encouraging insights from an experienced mother who incorporates the flow-parenting approach with her family.

Throughout the book, you will be delighted by the many illustrations of children and adults learning in flow.

YOU CAN PURCHASE FLOW TO LEARN
ON AMAZON, BARNES & NOBLE, and INGRAMS.

www.ingramcontent.com/pod-product-compliance
Lightning Source LLC
Chambersburg PA
CBHW031119080526
44587CB00011B/1036